A CLOSER LOOK AT *HARRY POTTER*

By the same author:

A CLOSER LOOK AT

Harry Potter

Bending and shaping the minds of our children

JOHN HOUGHTON

KINGSWAY PUBLICATIONS
EASTBOURNE

ISBN 0 85476 941 2

Published by
KINGSWAY PUBLICATIONS
Lottbridge Drove, Eastbourne, BN23 6NT, England.
Email: books@kingsway.co.uk

Designed and produced for the publishers by
Bookprint Creative Services, P.O. Box 827, BN21 3YJ, England.
Printed in Great Britain.

To Alistair and Debbie, Matthew and Sharon,
Steve and Emma,
who by love and prayer are training six to be wise.

'Those who are wise will shine
like the brightness of the heavens, and those
who lead many to righteousness, like the
stars for ever and ever.'
(Daniel 12:3)

Contents

Introduction

Imagine a baby narrowly escaping death in an assault that killed both his parents. The unfortunate infant is taken in with reluctance by the most appalling and bourgeois aunt and uncle that you could think of. They hate everything about him and conspire never to tell him his true identity. At the age of eleven the child is contacted out of the blue and told that he has a place at an exclusive boarding school somewhere in the north of Britain. Upon his arrival he makes his first real friends in life and together they have lots of fun. In the course of time they uncover a dark plot to steal a priceless jewel hidden in the school buildings. The would-be thief turns out to be none other than the person who murdered the child's parents and who now wants to complete the job by killing the boy.

Now, call the child Harry Potter and make him the gifted offspring of a witch and a wizard, who without his being aware of it is destined for a great future that is yet to be revealed. Introduce a complex society of witches skilled in the magic arts and operating secretively in a fantastical parallel world to our own – so close, however, that your neighbour down the street might easily be a practising member. Fill this plot with plenty of wit, and parody the 'people into frogs and flying broomsticks' notions of witch-craft while, at the same time, running a darker tale of good magic versus bad magic.

It turns out that Voldemort, the arch villain and mur-derer of Harry Potter's parents, was greatly weakened by his attempt to kill the baby, for the child had received some special and unexpected power from the death of his mother. However, rumour has it that Voldemort is seeking to re-establish himself and, although most of the witches in this society use magic for good purposes, some who have gone over to the Dark Side are helping him in his evil plans.

Harry Potter is at Hogwarts, a boarding school for young wizards. He travels there, along with other young witches, from platform nine and three quarters at Kings Cross, a magic doorway into a nostalgic world of steam trains, a forbidding lake and a turreted castle of great halls and secret passageways surrounded by a dark forest. The jewel is the philosopher's stone and Harry, with the help of his friends and the benevolent headteacher, faces and defeats the incarnation of Voldemort when he is mani-fested in a member of staff.

So begins the *Harry Potter* series by J. K. Rowling. So begins, too, the biggest children's book phenomenon of all time. To date, the first four out of the projected series of seven have broken all sales records, bringing delight to children, teachers, parents and publishers alike, and making the author a very wealthy and respected writer.

It all sounds like good clean fun, and good luck to the author. Yet while the world applauds, Christians are divided and many are calling for the books to be banned from state schools and public libraries. These are, after all, books about witchcraft, and the Scriptures make it clear that involvement with the occult is a serious no-no. Family Friendly Libraries (FFL) is scathing about the books: 'Harry is a warlock, his dad was a warlock and his mother was a witch', *and later,* 'the Harry Potter series focuses on the dark side of religion . . . the power is in self-centred pagan worship and magic, not in the righteous God of the world's great religions.'[1] FFL believes the books are inappropriate for reading in state schools.

Not all want to go that far. Taking a more tolerant view of the series, Lindy Beam, Youth Culture Analyst of Focus on the Family, states that 'children who read about Harry will probably discover little to nothing about the true world of the occult'. She quotes Charles Colson when he describes Rowling's magic as 'purely mechanical, as opposed to occultic'. Even so, she recognises that witchcraft is 'portrayed positively' and finds 'the spiritual fault of Harry Potter' to be not so much that 'it plays to the dark supernatural powers, but that it doesn't acknowledge any supernatural powers or moral authority at all'.[2]

With views like these doing the rounds it's hardly surprising that, in spite of the immense popularity of the books, Christian booksellers refuse to stock them.

According to reports and interviews at the Christian Booksellers Association convention 2000 held in New Orleans, the reasons given range from a policy of stocking only biblically based materials through to a concern that *Harry Potter* may provide an easy way into witchcraft.

The fact is, whatever we Christians say or do, our children will be hard put to avoid the *Harry Potter* phenomenon even if they want to. *Harry Potter* school projects, a further three volumes to come, a major film, games, merchandise, TV shows, websites – this is big business on a global scale and it can't be ignored.

It is the phenomenal sales and interest that requires us as Christians to take a closer look at *Harry Potter*, and even more so when the secular world appears to offer an uncritical acceptance of children's books about witches that deal with morality, spirituality and the conflict between good and evil. This is, after all, our territory and it is our job to pass comment on such matters!

Our aim in this book is to look at some of the key issues raised by the *Harry Potter* books – issues that every Christian parent, grandparent, aunt or uncle, Sunday school teacher, children's or youth worker and schoolteacher must understand if they are to raise up a Spirit-filled generation of children who love God and who love their neighbours. Those who want a simple unqualified condemnation of *Harry Potter* should look elsewhere; you will be disappointed. Those who wish to discern between good and evil in our current generation and who want to produce culturally literate, wise, godly children who know how to have fun without regrets and who can make a positive impact on their world, should read on. After all, someone is going to bend and shape the minds of our children.

John Houghton
January 2001

1
At Face Value

I think we should be grateful to J. K. Rowling. The *Harry Potter* books, with their mix of values and their wide appeal, provide us with one of the best opportunities we have had in years to exercise some discernment about the spirit of the age and to examine the relevance of the gospel message in the context of our contemporary culture.

To begin with, it is only right and proper that we should take the stories and their author at face value. Joanne Rowling is, without doubt, a gifted writer and one who has produced a series of very readable books that has a wide appeal among children and adults alike. She speaks of her own quite ordinary background with an engaging modesty. Born in Chipping Sodbury in Wiltshire, England, she attended Wyedean Comprehensive School before going on to Exeter University to study French. At the age of 26 she went abroad to teach English as a foreign language in Portugal. She married and had a daughter. Then life took a downturn and she found herself divorced and living on state benefit in Edinburgh, yet determined to finish the first *Harry Potter* novel. Her subsequent rise to fame is every aspiring author's dream: she moved from poverty to wealth thanks to a publisher who had the imagination to take a risk on a new writer and who was prepared to put a decent effort into good marketing. She greets the outstanding success of her work with wry bemusement.

The books themselves, aimed initially at the 8- to 14-year-old audience but read by many adults, are well crafted, entertaining, humorous and imaginative, and they make for a good read. Joanne Rowling has the rare gift of a fine writer: she stirs the imagination of the reader to picture what she is writing about. Her visual and comic style lets you see the grotesque Dursley family, the *olde worlde* steam train journey to the sombre castle, the moving figures in the portraits on the walls, the magical banqueting hall with its ever-changing ceiling, the wacky sky-borne game of Quidditch, the secret wizard street in London, Diagon Alley (diagonal ley – clever!), with its weird and wonderful shops – and plenty more besides.

She also writes something more than adventure stories, for her characters are not the predictable superheroes of Hollywood, zapping everyone in sight like intergalactic cowboys and Indians, with a few trite, sentimental clichés thrown in to give some pseudo-value to the action. Harry Potter's world is a moral one where lines are drawn between good and evil, and where good wins through in the end because of an underlying system of values that says it should. Further, the triumphs are not cheap; there is a price to pay, lessons have to be learned and choices must be made that carry consequences. As an example, when Harry is before the Sorting Hat he feels drawn to the nasty Slytherin House but he asks inside himself not to go there. He is put instead into the noble Gryffindor House. Dumbledore explains: 'It is our choices, Harry, that show what we truly are, far more than our abilities.'

This gives the tales an edge of realism. Harry Potter isn't perfect. He does tell lies and break the rules at times. His character is being formed as he learns to make right choices, and sometimes he gets it wrong. It is this very humanness that makes him so appealing, and which sets him in stark contrast to his Muggle guardians and those who serve the Dark Powers, both of whom alike lack humanity and virtue. Harry Potter is vulnerable, often indignant about his lot in life and feeling powerless in the face of events beyond his understanding. Many a child can identify with him.

There is a strong emphasis on the protective power of love too. Harry's parents had sacrificed their lives to save him when he was a baby and the memory of their devotion not only inspires him in his own battles but is the source of much of his power. His mentor, Dumbledore, says: 'To have been loved so deeply, even though the person who loved us is gone, will give us some protection for ever.' Christians should be at home with such a notion. Likewise, the loyal acceptance of Harry by the Weasley family and by his closest chums, Ron and Hermione, demonstrates the strength of real friendship and when that friendship is tested through misunderstanding it comes through stronger than ever.

It is this underlying quality that helps lift the books above the usual children's adventure story. For, although at one level this is a satire on the British public school story of yesteryear – and one that uses all the stereotyped characters of both staff and pupils and that is told with the engaging humour of Anthony Buckeridge's *Jennings* stories – at another level it is mythic and instructive. As with all who seek their holy grail Harry Potter is portrayed as a child of destiny who finds himself on a classical journey of self-discovery that mirrors so much of our own lives. Like all such travellers he is opposed by fierce adversaries, is challenged by stern guardians and receives help from wise mentors – yet always he must face his deepest trials and make his crucial choices by himself. The drama runs high; we all want to know what will become of our hero, and we all know that this will be decided more by the quality of his character than by the skills that he has acquired along the way.

Rowling's vivid world of the imagination, with its instant food, living portraits, magic sweets, passwords into secret places, crazy creatures, flying motor cars, hordes of gold, aerial sports with intelligent balls, and abracadabra wands, has one other thing going for it. It appeals to our 'if only' daydreams. Contrived with ingenuity and humour (her word plays on names are wonderful) it is great escapism!

But is it more? Such stories might have been conceived without recourse to witchcraft. As we shall see later, although the author has brought her own unique imagination to bear on the theme, the plot is not particularly new. Just as easily, Harry Potter could have discovered that he was the member of a special tribe or order who was destined to grow up as a liberator of the race. Once schooled in its culture and skills he could have faced his enemies with weapons that worked like magic but which were not in themselves magical. Advanced technology and the ingenuity of children could have provided all the necessary fun and sparkle along the way. The moral framework could have been just as clear and the imagination just as rich. There are many ways of telling such stories. So why use the world of witchcraft? Is there something more sinister going on, maybe some deliberate intention on the part of the author to lure children into the occult?

Some Christian fundamentalists seem to think so, and some have made fools of themselves, and done considerable harm to the credibility of the gospel, by quoting unsubstantiated, sensational nonsense drawn from X-rated satirical sources as though it were true. We should be ashamed of such folly; the world may malign us without integrity but we should not reply in kind.

Joanne Rowling has stated that she writes for the sheer pleasure of it. A storyteller from childhood, she wrote the first *Harry Potter* book because it was the kind of story she wanted to write. The entire concept for the series came fully formed into her mind, she says. Some Christian critics have immediately labelled this as occult impartation, akin to automatic handwriting, but in fact most authors of imaginative fiction have the same kind of experience. It is just the way the gift of storytelling works, and it is no more occult than an engineer envisaging, say, a Harrier jump jet or a Hovercraft. Neither of these novel machines was possible without the total picture first coming to birth in the imagination of the inventor. Indeed, as we shall see in the next chapter, this ability to see complete stories and structures is one of those characteristics that demonstrates the fact that we are made in the image of God, who himself conceived an entire universe before creating it.

Rowling herself has made it clear that she does not believe in the magic found in her books and has no intention of seducing children into witchcraft. In one interview she is quoted as saying: 'I am not trying to influence anyone into black magic. That's the very last thing I'd want to do . . . My wizarding world is a world of the imagination. I think it's a moral world.'[3]

That doesn't let the *Harry Potter* books off the hook by any means. The author may not have sinister intentions, but her work does provoke some real questions about the shifting values of our contemporary culture, and the degree to which it reflects and contributes to those values is worth examining.

Some of those changes are positive and others are quite disturbing, especially as they relate to our children. We need to understand what is being planted in their fertile imaginations and to ask what effect these things will have on their future lives. One thing is certain: they cannot grow up in a morally and spiritually neutral universe; that particular myth is well and truly scotched and only fools and bigots believe otherwise. Equally certain is the fact that our children will be more influenced by what goes into their imaginations than by any series of logical arguments, however well presented those may be. It is a tragedy that many Christians become uneasy at this point and so to this we must turn by taking a look at the phenomenon of imagination itself.

2

Just Imagine

It seems unlikely that earthworms engage in role-play
games or if they do they keep very quiet about it. Not so
some others of God's creatures; many animals have an
instinct to role play that is vital to their survival, whether it
be young stags practising head butts or lion cubs wrestling
with one another in the pride. This is how they learn to
defend themselves against predators, and how they develop their hunting skills. The family kitten with the ball of
wool is learning how to hunt mice, even though it will
probably only ever need to find its way to the bowl of
Kittychunks in the kitchen.

However, all this is based on instinct, not imagination.
Human children are different. Although, like the animals,
we do play games that teach us basic survival skills, such
as war dances or Monopoly – depending upon the needs
of our particular social grouping – we engage in another
level of play altogether, and it's because of who we are.

God has created us in his own image. This means we are the product of God's own imagination; what he saw in his mind, he made. It means too that we are a living image of what God is like; enter through the doorway of a human personality and you will find divine characteristics. These include the capacity for ideas, the use of language, the virtue of love – and imagination. Bearing this image is what makes us unique in creation and what drew the awed exclamation from the psalmist: 'What is man that you are mindful of him . . . ? You have made him a little lower than the heavenly beings and crowned him with glory and honour' (Psalm 8:4–5).

Being made in the image of the Imaginer, we have been granted this unique and amazing ability to imagine for ourselves. We can form pictures, or images, in our minds and by art and craft, and especially by words, convey those pictures to others so that they can see them in their own minds also. Take, for example, the following extract from *The Oswain Tales.*

A pale golden mist lay across the damp fields and the early morning sun hung low on the horizon, a disc of crimson fire that flashed burnished highlights on Sarah's blonde hair and kissed her honeyed skin with a blush of rose. Still warm from her slumbers, she opened the casement, smiled her serene smile, and breathed the cool air. It was sharp with the tang of early autumn, chilled cranberry sorbet all covered in wine. Rich russet leaves lay in curled flurries beneath the windless trees and spiders' webs heavy with sparkling dew hung like tiaras on the dark brambles. Somewhere across the marshes a flock of Canada geese rose in the dawn. Their faint mournful

cry carried over the mists and Sarah was filled with a soft sad-
ness for the memories of summers past.[4]

Creating these characters and their roles takes us beyond
survival or amusement. Our stories and images enable us
to reflect morally and spiritually about ourselves, and
without them we have neither civilisation nor society. The
Arts – painting, music, drama, architecture, sculpture and
storytelling – are the evidence of our humanity, the demonstration that we are made in the image of God. Monkeys
don't build cathedrals, recite Shakespeare or compose
symphonies.

This is why we humans cannot live without our stories,
whether real life or wholly imaginary, and why every society has its folklore complete with heroes and villains,
adventures and exploits, laws and lessons – and the more
vivid and stirring the better. In Western culture, old
favourites like Robin Hood teach us that government
should be challenged if it becomes tyrannous, the rich have
responsibilities to the poor, and the church should not be
the indulgent lackey of the state. Very English indeed, that!

The tales of King Arthur and his knights profoundly
shaped the notion of Christian chivalry, yet also reflected
the uneasy interplay between Christendom and paganism
in pre-scientific British culture. In these tales love, death
and destiny weave their complex pattern in a world still
trying to make up its mind about where the truth lies.

Cinderella reminds the downtrodden that miracles do
happen and dreams can come true. How many girls hope
for their Prince Charming as a result! We could go on: the

Grimm brothers' fairy tales and Aesop's fables, with their moral instruction and cautions; *Huckleberry Finn*, reflecting the uncertain transition of the American people into a nation; the plays of Shakespeare, or Dickens' *Oliver Twist* and *A Christmas Carol*, both of the latter affirming the process of social reform initiated by the mid-nineteenth-century Christian revival.

These images and story games help shape not only our own character but the national, and increasingly the international, character, so much so that today we can use a term like 'Western culture'. None of us escapes it: what we become in adult life is profoundly influenced by the images that we experience in our childhood and the emotional and spiritual impact that those images have on our minds. Nor does it stop with the onset of adolescence. What we are as adults continues to be shaped by the tales of our times. As a result, we will more easily believe the picture story in our heads than some new doctrine or notion, however logically presented, that fails to trigger a more powerful image in our minds – an observation not lost on the advertising industry.

So, in a world saturated not only with images but with a vast number of stories that spark the picture house of the mind, it is essential that we weigh the values and the impact that these have, not only on ourselves but also on our children. We dare not shirk our responsibility to protect the weak and the vulnerable, and children in particular who are at such a formative stage in their lives. Let their minds be bent and shaped the wrong way now and the damage will prove difficult if not well nigh impossible to remedy. We cannot simply sit them in front of the television or let them loose on the Internet; nor should we give them licence to read just anything they fancy simply because it is *in*. Since when could we trust the media to set the moral and spiritual tone of the nation?

Plain common sense recognises that children should be protected from violent or sexually explicit images, but even here the drift is apparent and far too many children are exposed to images and information that are beyond their capacity to handle in a healthy manner. Too many of us tend to trust the government-appointed watchdogs and guidelines rather than make the effort ourselves. It's a dangerous laziness, for we live in a world that operates on a value system very different from our own and for whom the word 'imaginative', like the word 'art', is a justification for almost anything.

The Bible makes it clear that imagination is far from neutral. There is such a thing as vain, or futile, imagination. Paul the apostle reminds us in the context of Romans 1:21 that be our idols of stone or steel, of sex or superstition or science, they have their origin in futile minds that have perverted the gift of God to serve lesser causes. One wonders what would have become of the theory of evolution had it remained in the realm of genuine science. In all likelihood it would have long been discarded as an inadequate explanation of origins. However, the vast investment in image-making by its proponents has lifted it to the level of myth and made it believable to the majority of the Western world – an apt fulfilment of Paul's words.

Since the world is given over to vanity, or futility, it is

hardly surprising that much of what it produces, unless moderated by something better, consists of negative and cynical images. We have only to note the obsession with violence, death and eroticism in our film and television industries so that even good plots nowadays have to contain obligatory blasphemy, killing and sex scenes. Why do they not contain an obligatory prayer, a gift to the poor and assistance to someone in need? Because life's not like that? But it is! Millions of people, and not just Christians, pray, give and assist others as part of their everyday lifestyle. But the producers work to a different agenda, don't they?

We can't just blame the producers of our mainline commercial media. The Internet with its assertion of human autonomy is replete with millions of pornographic and violent images, and many that are just plain sick. This is another fantasy world that feeds a vain imagination. Likewise, much of our contemporary literature has followed the same cynical trend and in so doing reduces our worth and experience to that of the dogs.

When it comes to media directed towards children there is considerably more restraint. Yet even here we find a world where Manga violence and quasi-sexual imagery are rampant, where witchcraft and sorcery are commonplace, and where ghosts and ghouls provide the entertainment and excitement rather than anything better.

Now, lest this seem too culturally negative we do well to remind ourselves that not by a long way is everything bad. Since 'every good and perfect gift is from above, coming down from the Father of the heavenly lights' (James 1:17), non-believers are well capable of producing works of great moral and spiritual worth. Indeed, some of the greatest artistic and imaginative achievements have come from professing unbelievers. In the West, nonetheless, much of that has arisen from a culture that has been profoundly influenced and shaped by a Christian worldview. Delivering people from the superstitions of idolatry, the Christian faith has enabled the creative gift to explore beauty without fear and to reflect upon human nature without explaining our behaviour simply in terms of the caprice of the gods or the activity of demons. It is a legacy that we neglect at our peril. Lose God and we lose our humanity; lose our humanity and we become programmed machines, or the habitation of demons.

Seldom has there been a greater need for Christians to engage positively and creatively in the imaginative arts. We do so in the great tradition of those who produced illuminated manuscripts, invented musical notation, designed the Sistine Chapel, built the cathedrals, painted the Dutch masters, wrote *Pilgrim's Progress*, produced the Authorised Version of the Bible; we include in our ranks all the great names – Bede, Erasmus, Haydn, Bach, Handel, Rembrandt, Tolstoy and many hundreds more, too numerous to mention – let alone the countless godly craftsmen and women who did and still do their work for the glory of God.

We must encourage the positive use of our imaginations. The apostle Paul advised us to watch over our thoughts: 'Whatever is true, whatever is noble, whatever is right, whatever is pure, whatever is lovely, whatever is admirable – if anything is excellent or praiseworthy – think about such things' (Philippians 4:8). This is no invitation to hide away from the harsh realities of life and even less to daub everything with crosses and doves; nor does it mean we must never listen to secular music or read non-Christian books or watch a Hollywood film. What it does urge, however, is that we look at life from a positive and redemptive perspective. The Bible story does not begin with sin, rebellion and evil; it begins with a God of love who made a beautiful world that was just full of goodness. Nor did the Fall spoil it all; God seriously limited the effects of evil and ensured that beauty would still remain and that we would aspire to find it. When history ends, it will do so with the return of the most beautiful Man who ever lived and who will inaugurate a splendid new creation in which all evil is banished. Can you imagine it? You should!

The least we can do for our children is to ensure that they know the greatest story ever told, for this will provide them with the means by which to judge all other tales when they encounter them. The divine drama is not only full of great tales in their own right, but the impact of those stories on the imagination helps shape a healthy worldview and provide the moral inspiration that children need in order to discern between good and evil.

Of course, they will have to face the full gamut of the world's images in the course of their lives and certainly as they grow into adulthood. No one can protect their children by hiding them away, and sets of rules or approved lists will do little other than make them either fearful in their imaginations or just longing to break the taboos to find out what is there.

This is the danger of treating the Bible merely as a set of theological propositions and proof texts. The Bible is a story book, a true story book, but none the less a narrative form through which God reveals himself and his will for the human race. All our proof texts must be seen in the wider context of the narrative. Those truly steeped in the Bible will have allowed its images and stories to shape their minds into seeing as God sees. They will not simply quote chapter and verse but rather, guided by the Holy Spirit and in fellowship with others, will develop the art of true discernment. The alternative seems to be the knee-jerk reaction of rigid fundamentalism and it is motivated far more by fear than by truth. What our children need is to learn the true wisdom that comes from above, and to learn it in the narrative form that parallels the way in which they have to live their own lives.

It would be a grave mistake and a theological error to restrict our children's reading to the Bible, or even to just 'Christian' books. They need access to the wealth of good reading that we have available to us – books that inspire the imagination and encourage a positive and caring lifestyle. These don't have to be just *nice* stories. Indeed, we may do more harm than good by restricting their reading to books that fail to do justice to the realities of life. The Bible is never like that! Children do need to know about hatred and injustice, about suffering and disease, about conflict and victory, about hope and despair, about life and death. What they don't need is literature that is selfish and cynical at heart or that encourages a pathological gloom

31

about life before ever they have had a chance to appreciate its beauties.

Why recommend books in an age of television, film, computer games and Web surfing? Simply because good books, like radio stories, stimulate the imagination far, far better than film or television can ever do. Words create images in our minds, whereas the televisual and cinematic media merely give us someone else's picture. Who has not been disappointed with a film rendition of a favourite book simply because the images projected on the screen are nowhere near as good as the ones in our heads? Whatever you hear to the contrary, the fact is that more people than ever before are curling up with a bit of processed tree and printer's ink and loving every minute of it. The book is far from dead!

Wise parents and teachers will encourage the imagination of the children in their charge. They will ask about the images that come into their heads. Some may seem silly or childish to us, but that is perhaps because we have settled into a way of looking at life that no longer allows for a freshness of approach. We should respect our children's own ways of seeing things and avoid the temptation to dismiss their ideas as foolish, otherwise they will learn never to indulge their secrets with us, and that is simply asking for trouble. The tale of a man with a thousand boots to put on his feet dreamed up by one of our grandchildren during a recent car journey may have been wacky but it led to all sorts of discussions about time and practicality and why it was probably best that God gave us just two legs!

How much should we protect children from the effects of their imaginations? That will depend to a large extent on the sensitivity of the individual child. However, some books, like some TV programmes, are simply not going to be good for them because the material is intrinsically evil. Others will be suitable only when a child has reached a sufficient stage of emotional development to handle the content. An underdeveloped mind will not be able to cope with the overloaded imagination. This is what often causes bad dreams and nightmares.

If we find that our children are being disturbed or if their behaviour pattern is being affected by what they have read, we should quickly censor any further involvement. We should also pray with them about whatever it is that is upsetting them. It is one thing to read about ghosts, but it is quite another to be left with a ghost in the imagination.

Many years ago we prayed for a girl who at too young an age saw the 1930s version of *King Kong* (by far the scariest in our opinion). That night the gorilla walked through her bedroom wall and entered her head. From that time onwards she suffered from severe epilepsy, complete with the characteristic dip in the brain scan printout. One of her parents brought her to our church years later and we prayed for her deliverance. Her epilepsy disappeared, and the brain scans returned to normal. Now we are not suggesting that this is the cause and cure of all cases of epilepsy, but the point is that we do need to be aware of what is taking place in our children's imaginations and we do need to be wise over what we allow them to read or view lest they become prey to every opportunistic spirit and wind of doctrine that blows their way.

Sci-fi and fantasy are particularly powerful forms of literature since they invoke entire worlds of the imagination quite unlike our own. Fantasy also addresses the subconscious mind, especially if it is based on a mythic structure, as we will see in the next chapter. It has a great power for good, but also for evil if it is of the wrong kind. The *Harry Potter* stories fall into this genre of literature.

We will examine the good and bad points of these stories in the pages that follow but suffice it to state right now that in our opinion the power and the darkness of the imagery, and the graphic and at times gory scenes, makes these unsuitable reading for most children below the age of ten. Parents of highly impressionable children may wish to restrict the books to an even later age, especially as the author has indicated that the darkness and violence of the plots is likely to increase in the subsequent volumes.

Imagination is one of the finest gifts that God has bestowed upon us. All major scientific discoveries, all social and political reforms come about because of its use. Martin Luther King's famous words say it all: 'I have a dream . . .' We should nurture and encourage our children to dream, to imagine a better world. With God's help, they may just go on to produce it.

3
Myths and Magic

No stories have greater power on the imagination than those built around what we call mythic structure. Such stories include the old legends of King Arthur, and Odysseus, and the voyages of Sinbad. Modern examples that follow the same pattern include *The Lord of the Rings*, *The Wizard of Oz* and *Star Wars*.

It's a pattern that goes something like this: a very ordinary person is called to make a heroic journey to save the world. He accepts the call reluctantly, not believing the special secret about his real identity. A wise mentor appears and gives him advice. He crosses the threshold into the realm of high adventure and soon faces stern guardians who have to be bribed, impressed or silenced. There he finds magic weapons to help him. A series of trials follows in which he will be helped by various allies. Somewhere in the background will lurk a sinister shadow. All this will prepare him for the supreme ordeal, often in the form of a goddess figure, where he must fight alone. If he overcomes the test he will obtain the elixir of life. The hero must then return to his own people. This is not easy and he will flinch at the journey. However, help will come, often by means of flight, and the hero will return to his own world. When he does so, he will be master of both realms, for his journey has proved to be one of self-discovery, and it has made him a man. In the words of Aldous Huxley, 'The man who comes back through the Door in the Wall will never be quite the same as the man who went out.'[5]

Myths may or may not be based on historical truth, but they contain profound truths about human existence, and therein lies their power. We are all on a journey called life; from the ordinariness of childhood, we must face the trials and uncertainties of growing up. Along the way we will make some friends and face some enemies. We will master some skills and face our shadowy fears. At some point we may encounter a decisive challenge to our future. Many fail at this encounter and they pay the price, which is to enter adulthood emotionally trapped in adolescence. Nowhere is this more apparent in our society than in sexual relationships. So many people bowing to sexual allure outside of marriage become incapable of sustaining a marital relationship in adult life. Instead, like pubescent teenagers, they keep 'falling in love' without ever passing the test that enables them really to love as only a grown-up can.

Whatever the test and however the test is framed, those who succeed are rewarded with emotional adulthood and, be it as mundane as earning a living and raising a family, they make their contribution to the good of society. For most of us, better be a little hero than no hero at all.

Mythic tales help us live out our journey vicariously; that is, we see ourselves, and learn, through someone else's experience. In the success of the hero we find hope for our own uncertain path. We desperately want Frodo Baggins to cast the ring into the cracks of doom, because if he fails, what hope is there for the rest of us? If Frodo cannot defeat evil, will evil prove to be the stronger force after all?

Thus we face our inner terrors and dream our dreams. If the myth is doing its job it will inspire us to higher ideals and teach us its morals. Its ancestral archetypes – those ancient figures of fairy tales and enchantment – touch us deep inside; the metaphors and symbols fire our imaginations, so much so that they become the unconscious foundations of our lives. Such myths shape our value system and our worldview, and they shape who we will become.

It is at once obvious that the *Harry Potter* books are based on mythic structure. Each volume in itself is a mini-myth but each is part of the larger myth of the ongoing plot. Harry the hero, like Dorothy in *The Wizard of Oz*, enters a parallel world. There he begins his dark journey to face the shadow in his past, to deal with both the blessing and the curse of his origins. Dumbledore is his wise mentor and Ron, Hermione and Hagrid are among his allies. Snape and McGonagall are gatekeepers; Malfoy is the trickster; and Voldemort the shadow. Shapeshifters abound. Although we have only four volumes to date, it is fairly clear what direction the plot must take and what the final outcome is likely to be (though it would be a pity to spoil the fun by making suggestions at this stage). This being so, the *Harry Potter* series is capable of exercising a profound influence on young minds. The question is whether the influence will be for good or for ill.

For many Christians the answer is simple: ban myth altogether. The word is too closely associated with falsehood, and such stories are too dangerous and disturbing. Give us safe, logical facts, solid scientific proof texts, systematic theology, and the 'real' stories of the Bible.

The concern is understandable, but wrongly placed. First, myth, in this context, means anything but falsehood. It is a true story pattern that is modelled on the realities of life. Second, the safe, logical, unimaginative approach is not biblical. The Bible itself is a narrative that is largely based on a mythic structure. We should expect this, since God's word is truth and must relate to the realities of our human experience. It also contains the mythic (not mythical) exploits of characters like Joseph and, above all, the life of Christ. As we read the Gospels we discover all the key elements of myth portrayed in the greatest story ever told. Little wonder it should be such a captivating and compelling story. The Holy Spirit himself has inspired the form as well as the words!

We want to avoid any confusion at this point: the mythic form of the Scriptures allows us to call it myth but it is not make-believe, folk legend or fiction. These events really happened in our space-time continuum, they are historically true and culminated in the Word becoming flesh and dwelling among us, full of grace and truth (John 1:14). The

Bible writers are careful to ensure that we understand this: 'We did not follow cleverly invented stories when we told you about the power and coming of our Lord Jesus Christ, but we were eye-witnesses of his majesty' (2 Peter 1:16). When the Bible reads as if historically true, we take it that it is.

The point of the incarnation and of all the rest of the Bible narrative is that God reveals himself through the story of people's lives. We do well to remember this, because much of our failure to communicate the gospel effectively in our postmodern world is a failure to recognise the importance of telling the story. Yet Paul himself, the most 'theological' of writers, drew constantly from the narrative of the Old Testament as well as from the life of Christ. The book of Romans, for example, cannot be understood without knowing the heroic journey of faith lived out by Abraham. How tragic that we should reduce this story to a few proof texts on the subject of justification by faith. Neat, logical, uninspiring; people go away without a narrative to fire their imaginations, and little wonder then that a vivid film, or even a soap opera, can wipe away the neat list of facts presented by the preacher *quod erat demonstrandum*. Which is perhaps why we feel it necessary to deliver the same thing in a different wrapping the next week!

In truth, our down playing of the imagination and our obsession with linear logic owes more to the rationalism of the Enlightenment than to the Scriptures. Yet even science depends upon the imagination and upon stories for its progress. The clockwork universe, the big bang theory, the theory of evolution; all the science developed around such notions is based on images and narratives – and not necessarily true ones either!

So, accepting that the Bible is a mythic narrative, should we stick to that alone? At least we can trust the word of God! While we should certainly steep ourselves and our children in the Scriptures, we should recognise two scriptural truths. First, God bestows common grace on all of humanity. So passionate is God about reconciling the world to himself that he accustoms us to his character through the many blessings of creation and culture alike. The world is littered with clues that point us unerringly in the direction of Christ: 'Great are the works of the LORD; they are pondered by all who delight in them' (Psalm 111:2); 'You open your hand and satisfy the desires of every living thing' (Psalm 145:16). God himself

> gives all men life and breath and everything else. From one man he made every nation of men, that they should inhabit the whole earth; and he determined the times set for them and the exact places where they should live. God did this so that men would seek him and perhaps reach out for him and find him, though he is not far from each one of us. (Acts 17:25–27)

Second, God uses unbelievers in his purposes, be they Baalam's ass, the pagan king Cyrus, 'my anointed', or the writers that Paul quotes on Mars Hill. This has led Christian thinkers like C. S. Lewis and many others to acknowledge that pagan writings can and do contain elements of truth that help us in our journey towards salvation. *Lord of the Flies*, for example, is one of the most powerful expositions of the reality of the fall of man and of the corruption of sin. *Terminator 2* is a vivid portrayal of the relentlessness of sin, the need for a Saviour and the necessity of a sacrifice to destroy evil, with much of its plot line reflecting the symbolism of Revelation 12.

If we accept the power and place of mythic stories, not only for their insights into the mystery of human existence but also because of their common grace potential to guide us in our search for reality, then we must judge such tales not just for historical accuracy or literary integrity but for their psychological, moral and spiritual accuracy too.

It is impossible to characterise mythic tales as simply good or bad. Always there will be a mixture and we will need to exercise our own discernment (more of that later). *The Lord of the Rings*, for instance, would rate highly with many Christians because of its fine moral tone and redemptive pattern. Yet it is also ultimately depressing: the golden age is past, the future mundane, and the notion of the afterlife is shrouded in the mists of uncertainty. These are hardly Christian notions!

We should certainly look for redemptive patterns in stories; good must win in the end, and where it doesn't then the reasons must be apparent. In the great Bible story of Saul and David, the reasons for Saul's failure are made clear, as they are too for David's victories and his shortcomings. Cynical tales would simply put it down to luck, and that is certainly the case with the interactive books and CDs where the reader fights the enemy with no sense of moral superiority and learns nothing except that he was

41

lucky to survive this time. Such stories truly are best left on the shelves.

The *Star Wars* myth, while containing many good elements, raises another kind of issue – that of worldview. In the case of *Star Wars* it is a Taoist/Buddhist view of reality where a yin/yang Force can be tapped into for good or ill, depending upon your personal predisposition. Such a view is in flat opposition to the Bible and those Christians who likened the Force to the Holy Spirit could hardly have been more wrong. Many of our questions about *Harry Potter* are to do with the worldview portrayed by the author.

What if those myths contain elements of magic and enchantment? This is a prominent feature in the *Harry Potter* stories and one that in itself has been sufficient for some Christians to avoid the books. Do those same Christians also avoid the enchanting tale of Cinderella with her fairy godmother and magic pumpkin coach, or Snow White and the Seven Dwarfs?

We need to distinguish between magic performed as a serious exercise of power and magic as a storyteller's symbol for life and transformation. In the case of Cinderella it is clearly the latter: her inner goodness in spite of her ill-use, her higher aspirations, her hopes and dreams, are rewarded by a magical experience that changes her life. We should not be afraid of this use of the term and when the teenager says, 'Jesus is magic!' he is quite right!

The issues are far more serious when it comes to manipulative magic. In real life the Bible condemns sorcery and all those who engage in the magic arts, whether they be the

Egyptian magicians in the time of Moses, or the Babylonian magicians in Daniel's day, or the sorcerers in Israel, or any others. Revelation 22:15 bans such from the city of life: 'Outside are . . . those who practise magic arts.' At the heart of this kind of magic is a way of doing life without reference to God; a belief that we can manipulate the forces or the demons in order to better ourselves or others.

This is a form of idolatry. It is all very well for those who practise so-called 'white magic' to claim that they have no malice in their rituals compared to those who do 'black magic', but that is missing the point. Ritual magic itself is wrong, irrespective of the claimed motives of its practitioners. To steal from a neighbour to help someone in need may be a more noble motive than undisguised thievery but it doesn't justify stealing. There are more legitimate ways of aiding a needy cause.

In *Harry Potter* we have two elements running side by side: a comic one where the author, in a Disneyesque fashion, parodies the classic stereotypes of magic, and another darker element where magic is used as a weapon by both the good guys and the bad guys. While we may accept that the lessons in trivial spell-casting are a humorous parallel to learning general sciences in the real world, we cannot avoid the connection between this and the use of magic as a means of control and intimidation; one surely leads to the other in these books. Such a use in our world, even for good purposes, is unacceptable. Yet already in the *Harry Potter* books there is an overlap between the two realms. It seems unavoidable that Harry will use magic in the non-wizard world and, in fact, he does so on his aunt and uncle and their son, Dudley. Because they are portrayed as such revolting creatures we are led to approve of Harry's actions on a 'serves them right' basis.

The magic in *Harry Potter* is not magical or enchanting in the fairy tale sense, and the good stuff is not a symbol for life. These are sombre books about the exercise of power rather than personal transformation, serious stuff to do with the conflict between good and evil. It would be foolish to suggest that every reader of these books will be tempted to become a magician, but it is equal folly to imagine that no one will. At least some will try to use spells either as a defence against people or events that threaten them, or as a form of malice or revenge against others.

Christians have a better answer to both these situations. For those who are afraid we recommend prayer to the living God whose perfect love casts out fear. For those who are vindictive we recommend repentance from the sin of not loving their neighbour.

The rising interest in magic is not accidental. None of us can live long for scientific materialism alone. Our lives cry out for meaning, for enlightenment, for spirituality. Historically, that has been found, to use C. S. Lewis' phrase, in the 'deeper magic' of the cross of Christ, 'the Lamb slain from the creation of the world'. This is the truly old religion of which paganism is but a later and diseased offshoot. However tentatively Western man sets out on the road back to spirituality he will sooner or later be faced with a fork where he must choose to 'know the mystery of

God, namely, Christ, in whom are hidden all the treasures of wisdom and knowledge' (Colossians 2:2–3) or he will descend into witchcraft.

4
Talking of Witches

Arthur Miller's play, *The Crucible*, reminds us that paranoia can make witches out of any one of us. In his explanation of the phenomenon, which he calls 'daemonism', Miller suggests that a combination of disappointed hopes, inexplicable failures and superstitious fear gives rise to the need to find scapegoats rather than to look for more rational and responsible explanations for our ills. His warning is well founded and Christians as well as governments are wise to take note; they may have been grossly exaggerated, but we are still living down the evil legacy of those medieval witch-hunts.

Witch-hunting is a sign of weakness and when the world perceives our knee-jerk reactions to be driven by fear it concludes that our faith is too shallow to stand scrutiny or to survive the real world in which people often seem to make a better job of life than do Christians themselves. Robust faith will not see demons under every rose bush, nor will it be blown around by the latest passing fads of our tragicomic culture. The church of Jesus Christ across the globe daily takes on far greater obstacles and overcomes them by the word of God and the blood of the Lamb – often at the cost of heroic self-sacrifice and with a rough-hewn nobility of character that puts Christians' cowardly opponents to shame. Truly, 'the world was not worthy of them'. However, find the right cause for which to die, Christians. *Harry Potter* isn't one of them.

That said, *Harry Potter* is about active witches and wizards. He is a warlock and his parents are a warlock and a witch. We don't have to go hunting for witches – in this case, they are intrinsic to the plot. It is, then, perfectly legitimate for us as morally and spiritually responsible people to make an assessment of the witchcraft theme in these stories. To do so, we must look at the role of the witch in literature and folklore, and the reality of witchcraft in the world today.

Perhaps the most subtle and subconscious literary use of the witch is to represent the dark side of motherhood. In this instance the witch figure is often a shapeshifter, and may alternate between appearing as a figure of compassion and as a tyrant; for it is in the power of a mother to provide nurture and protection but also to deny the same either out of caprice or to force the child to grow up. In psychological terms this use of the witch motif refers back to the time of a child's weaning and to those apron string ties by which a child is both protected by a mother but also subject to her will. In mythic tales, the hero overcomes the tyrant's control and becomes an adult able freely to choose his own destiny. In real life, once having released ourselves from the apron strings, we can then love our mothers by free choice. Such a usage can be seen reflected in the legends of King Arthur and in the first of my Oswain Tales, *Oswain and the Shadow-Witch of Alamore.*

Closely allied to this usage, and perhaps appealing more to girls, is the witch as representing fear of the future, particularly for those who have lost one or both of their parents. The wicked stepmother becomes the archetypal image of the witch because she exercises power without love over the child's life and is herself often jealous of the child's youth, beauty and claim to her father's affection. Nowhere is this better portrayed than in *The Wizard of Oz.* Snow White and the Seven Dwarfs demonstrates a similar usage and in both instances, with the help of friends, the heroines discover the inner resources that they need to overcome their fear. Of the older stories, Hansel and Gretel is probably the most powerful tale of the witch representing archetypal fear.

Related to the debunking of fear is the comic usage of the witch, as in *The Sorcerer's Apprentice* and in the sitcom *Bewitched.* Here witches are fallible, human like us, their spells mostly go wrong, and even if they do work there is probably another explanation for why they appear to do so. Laughter is a great antidote to fear – a lesson we do well to learn and one that Harry Potter is encouraged to grasp also.

The witch may also be a representation of wisdom, as with Merlin in the tales of King Arthur or Gandalf in *The Lord of the Rings.* This traces back to the original meaning of the word 'occult', which referred to the academic study of esoteric mysteries needing an explanation, rather than to participating in seances and the like. In this sense too the witch can be an instructor. Curses work because people have committed folly. This might be an error of morality or a failure of common sense. Either way, it is human error that gives ground for the spell to work. Tommy playing with matches might well allow the fire-witch to burn the house down!

The witch may, of course, be a symbol for genuine evil, indeed for Satan himself, as is the case in *The Lion, the Witch and the Wardrobe*, where malice, manipulation and magic combine with deception to create a monstrosity that expresses the reality of spiritual evil personified. In C. S. Lewis' tale, only a redemptive sacrifice can overcome the devil, and the parallel with Christ's death and resurrection is easily drawn.

One other popular usage of the witch today is the political one, where witches engage in a battle for power using supernatural powers of psychological and physical manipulation. Such a use includes the non-occultic shapeshifters like *Superman* and superheroes in general, as well as *Batman* and *The Invaders*, the latter a thinly disguised anti-Communist series if ever there was one! It also includes localised and more witchy manipulators like *Lizzie Dripping* and *Buffy the Vampire Slayer*. In all these cases, ordinary mortals are at the mercy of the bad witches and can only be saved by the intervention of the good witches. We shall return to the implications of such conditioning.

All this is a far cry from real witchcraft, the history of

which can be traced back biblically to that associated with the fertility cults of Canaan and the magicians of Egypt and Babylon. So dangerous was this occult activity considered to be that the death penalty was prescribed under the Law of Moses: 'Do not allow a sorceress to live' (Exodus 22:18); 'Let no-one be found among you who sacrifices his son or daughter in the fire, who practises divination or sorcery, interprets omens, engages in witchcraft' (Deuteronomy 18:10).

We are talking here of serious occult practices, decidedly dark magic that opened people up to the reality of demon possession. This was more than a matter of superstitious fear ruling people's lives; it also engaged them in sexual immorality, idol worship and child sacrifice. Little wonder that the Mosaic law sought to ban such activities. Indeed, it was a failure to heed those instructions that led the Israelites into eventual captivity. Essential to a belief in monotheism and the morality that flows from it is a renunciation of all forms of occult activity. Finally shaking off their polytheism, the post-captivity Jews were able to pave the way for the coming of the Messiah and to make possible the spiritual liberation of the whole world.

For this reason, the New Testament is no less adamant that witchcraft has to go. While it does not call for the death penalty and indeed offers instead salvation to witches who repent (e.g. Simon Magus in Acts 8:9–24, and the Ephesian believers in Acts 19:18–20), none the less the unrepentant are among those consigned to the second death (see Revelation 21:8).

Jesus came to reveal a loving heavenly Father who is not

far from any one of us, and who is a very present help in time of trouble. His ministry on earth was not only compassionate, it was immensely powerful. When we read the life of Christ we enter a world where inner demons are vanquished, the sick are healed, miracles abound, the powerless are given hope and through knowing Christ the door to the spiritual Holy of Holies is flung wide to welcome people into communion with the mystery of God himself.

If that were not enough, the ascent of Christ to the right hand of the Father not only set him above all other spiritual and mortal beings in the universe but heralded the outpouring of the Holy Spirit upon his church. The work that Jesus began, he continues through his people. All across the world the proclamation of the good news brings peace and certainty regarding the future. Angels intervene, demons still flee at the name of Jesus, the sick continue to be healed, the bereft find solace, the poor begin the process of transforming their lives, mercy is ministered to millions. If Christians withdrew their goodwill, society would collapse overnight.

True, none of this is an easy path but it is the path to eternal life, and better that than the tragic alternative. The living word of God proclaimed in prophetic power and exemplified in transformed lives that call on the name of Jesus, is the greatest 'spell' of all; the priestly celebration of the Lord's Supper by believers recalls and makes present a 'holy magic' that renders all other sacrifices null and void; the apostolic authority of the name of Jesus Christ on the lips of God's people declares that there is one Lord and one alone, who will some day return to judge the living and the dead.

Unlike mere religion, there is no hierarchy of merit among true believers. The lowliest Christian may pray with the authority of Christ, the gifts of the Holy Spirit are tools granted even to the apprentices of faith, the least recognised are seated with Christ in the heavenly places, 'far above all rule and authority, power and dominion, and every title that can be given' (Ephesians 1:21). We have a better way. Who needs witchcraft and its pale substitutes?

Evidently, many think they do. Humans want for supernatural help; of that there is little doubt. For all the wonders of modern science and medicine, we remain vulnerable creatures beset by fears and uncertainties, subject to accidents and ills and knowing no more of the future than we did a thousand years ago. Christians may declare that supernatural help comes 'from the LORD, the Maker of heaven and earth' (Psalm 121:1–2), and not from the hills upon which we make our futile offerings or from which we hope to draw on some earth magic, yet in practice the Western church appears to be powerless, lacking the spirituality that people crave, and failing to address the real issues in their lives. Despairing of a materialistic church, people in need are increasingly likely to turn to a witch rather than to a saint. Indeed, it seems easier to believe in UFOs and extraterrestials than in angels.

There is little doubt that the profoundly evil side of witchcraft flourishes today and that it involves ritual killing and gross human degradation, much of it well outside the law of the land, let alone the law of God. Much

more popular, however, is middle-class ecological paganism. This is the stuff of women's magazines and evening
classes, of correspondence courses and 'Mind, Body, Spirit'
sections in bookshops; it is the world of discreet covens
practising their rituals and making their offerings, net-
working for peace and healing through astral projection,
chanting their mantras and, as latter-day animists, contact-
ing the elemental spirits of nature.

For some it has evolved into a formalised neo-pagan religion known as Wicca that meets in covens of initiates as
regularly and religiously as any church. Much of this is of
recent invention based upon dubious historical claims
about the survival of ancient underground paganism.
Modern Druidism, for example, owes its origins to John
Toland in 1717 but likes to claim older roots.

Closely bound up with all this is the New Age
Movement with its emphasis on Gaia, the Mother Earth,
and the discovery of the god within. This is little more than
a return to pantheism through a variety of techniques bor-
rowed from across the world and Westernised to become
another form of consumerism.

Meanwhile, at the level of popular culture, millions
indulge in the superstitious ritual of their daily horoscope,
carry lucky crystals, dabble in seances and Ouija boards
and much else besides. Witchcraft, the desire to manipulate our destiny and the destiny of others, has seldom been
more prevalent.

So, what are we to make of the witchcraft of *Harry
Potter*? That such a series of books should be written
should hardly come as a surprise given the culture in

which we find ourselves. How then shall we categorise it?

In the light of our literary analysis earlier in this chapter, it falls into the twin categories of the comic stereotype and the political manipulation of power. There is nothing very profound about the parodies of popular representations of witchy activities with the misfiring spells and magic sweets, nor even the surreal notions of wizard banks full of gold guarded by goblins (a version of the gnomes of Zurich?). Pouring scorn on such notions of magic is a very effective way of dismissing it to make way for something stronger.

For this is not simply a comic tale serving to debunk popular witchcraft or even to assuage our fears of such superstitions. The fun side is of a continuum with the more serious side. The teachers at Hogwarts can do real magic; their spells are powerful and they work. It is to be expected that their students will graduate to the same or higher levels. The adult witches can also use their magic on the Muggles, or non-witches, that make up ordinary society. That is to say nothing of those who are on the Dark Side and, although a moral distinction is drawn between good and bad wizardry, it is not always well drawn. There is no question but that the good guys need to become proficient at the same sorts of magic used by the bad guys. In this respect *Harry Potter* is about as far removed from Narnia or Oswain as it is possible to be.

Harry Potter presents us with an uneasy spectrum of occult and magic practice that ranges from the frivolous to the truly evil and macabre. It raises the question about where the line is to be drawn. Although some of the characters can be clearly identified as going over to the Dark Side, it is assumed that all the rest are by default on the side of light, yet there is no authority for the light side to exist, no reason why it should be so. Even the wizard laws imposed by that parody of Whitehall, the Ministry of Magic, have no basis or appeal to any higher authority.

While the author has made it clear that she has no intention of seducing anyone into black magic, given this absence of justification for the light side, there is no compelling reason to stop anyone who starts on the occult slope from sliding further than they planned. Children are highly suggestible; they are also prone to their own terrors and nightmares. By putting a smiling face on some aspects of witchcraft, yet failing to draw a proper moral line, it is too easy for children to experiment, not knowing that in the real world ritual games can, for the vulnerable, lead to a good deal of trouble. How far do you plunge your hand into a dark hole before whatever lurks there bites it? And if it does, what price will you have to pay for it to let go?

Morality without a message, and a message without an author, is ultimately unsustainable. Harry Potter, following his own instincts, will break the laws of the Ministry of Magic or the school rules where occasion demands, simply on the grounds of his innate feelings. That kind of autonomy is dangerous. When everyone does what is right in their own eyes it is the end of civilisation and society. Anarchy builds no roads; only barricades.

Children today are the offspring of parents steeped in situation ethics. Those parents believed that all you needed was love, yet they interpreted love to mean pleasure, notably sexual pleasure, while pretending that it was something virtuous. Today's kids have no such pretensions. The message now is 'All I need is what I want'. If Harry Potter can break the rules, so can I.

The proponents of the so-called Age of Aquarius want to tell us that this is no longer a problem. In their cuckoo world there is no conflict; all is one. Children, and for that matter adults, are innately good. Simply respond to the inner light and conjoin with the Force and all will be well. The only sin is not being yourself; the only demons are those created by the unenlightened.

Would that it were that simple. Take away any ultimate authority for good and evil and our actions boil down to the manipulation of events and people for our own self-interest. Whoever has the best technology wins. As John Andrew Murray has written, contrasting J. K. Rowling with C. S. Lewis:

> Rowling's work invites children to a world where witchcraft is 'neutral' and where authority is determined solely by one's might or cleverness. Lewis invites them to a world where God's authority is not only recognised, but celebrated – a world that resounds with his goodness and care.[6]

Harry Potter's world reflects the secular–pagan mentality that, because it has rejected God's authority in favour of political expediency, has given us such horrors as nuclear weapons and chemical and bacteriological warfare, let alone the obscenity of ethnic cleansing and the poverty brought about by exploitive multinationalism. If you can't draw the line spiritually, you can't draw the line at all, and we are left at the mercy of the power freaks in the playground.

The Bible, by contrast, defines an unmistakable moral line with reference to God himself. There is a kingdom of darkness and there is an overarching kingdom of God's own Son. Much as we may liken our lives to a spiritual journey, there remains a definite point where we cross the immutable line from one kingdom to the other. Christians commonly call this conversion. That line is not fixed by our innate feelings or by some other arbitrary authority. It originates from the living God himself, from none less than the Righteous Judge of all the earth.

The world of *Harry Potter* is devoid of this transcendence; there is nothing for which to aspire, no numinous awe in the presence of goodness, no supreme Other to be sought after or worshipped, no Person to love. Thus, the witchcraft consists of little more than materialistic and psychological manipulation, while failing to reflect reality. In denying the truly spiritual it presents a false worldview, and to this we must now turn.

5

Worlds Apart

At one time we believed that the Earth was the centre of the universe and the sun and the planets orbited around it while also performing mini-orbits of their own. This complicated and quite wrong view of the solar system was developed by the humanist Claudius Ptolemy, from ideas proposed by Pythagoras. People believed it for twelve hundred years until around AD 1500 when a Christian, Nicolaus Copernicus, proved that the planets, including Earth, orbit the sun. This major change of model, or paradigm shift, has had a profound effect on Western culture. Today, secular man is lost in space. No longer the centre of everything, he now wonders if he is anything at all. One simple realisation has altered radically the way we see the whole of reality. We have changed our worldview.

Our worldview is the grid through which we interpret our experiences; it is a set of ideas and assumptions that helps us make sense of life. Changing one or more of these assumptions is akin to receiving sight for the first time. For example, it was believed by a majority of the population that black people were a subhuman species; this being so, there was no reason why they could not be harnessed like animals and put to work. Christian evangelists proved that black slaves responded to the gospel. It was an eye-opener and the implication was unavoidable: black people have human souls, they must be emancipated, and we must ask their forgiveness. That paradigm shift led to the abolition of slavery and to the establishment of the UN Charter and the European Convention on Human Rights. We have a different worldview as a result.

The reason why many Christians are unsure about the *Harry Potter* books is not simply because of the plot or even the use of magic (though they might think so) but because of their underlying worldview. To make sense of this we need to understand the important changes that are taking place in our society – changes that are leading us towards a worldview that we as Christians are called to challenge at its very root.

First, the scientific worldview is on the wane. This is not the same as saying that science is dying; it is simply that as a way of interpreting reality thoughtful people are finding it increasingly inadequate. A logical nothing-but-ism that reduces our existence to patterns of electrochemical impulses whose random effects grant us the illusion of freedom just doesn't do justice to our humanity. Scientists who still teach this have become a bore and their ideas something of a joke. The human spirit cries out for something more and knows it is there. Indeed, our focus on information technology suggests that the universe is information; yet all intelligent information originates from someone. Arguably there is an Informer behind the information. Why did that Informer make us capable of receiving it, and what does it mean?

Second, existentialism is ceasing to be! As a reaction to scientific determinism it proved inadequate. 'Now' experiences to authenticate our being have not produced a warm caring society of spiritually sensitive people. Instead, it has hardened into individualism and consumerism and its rock gurus are now just plain rich. Our craving for instant fulfilment has made us the slaves of a push-button technology that grants us sensation without meaning and cost without value. The child of the science against which we rebelled has become our master.

Third, cultural Christianity is a spent force. There are still plenty of old world Christians around but either they have retreated into the ghetto or they have so imbibed the surrounding culture that they no longer have anything distinctive to offer. Introverted and apologetic, and having no viable apologetic, such Christianity no longer informs the public debate. All that remains is a sort of pragmatic morality – common sense without Christ – that keeps society functioning but which requires more and more legislation and state spying to make it work. Behaviour is no longer constrained by grace but by CCTV cameras.

Old world cultural churches will continue to exist as a monument to the past, much as Guy Fawkes Night or the last night of the Proms. TV evangelists can be assured of a wealthy livelihood, and middle-class respectability will ensure suburban congregations, but they are irrelevant to the real world – mere consumers of popular culture trailing pathetically in the wake of the world's agenda and offering a belated Christian version to a world that has already made up its mind.

The passing of these three great worldviews is what gives us the postmodern world. Although the tides will continue for some time to wash around the sinking islands of the past, a new island is arising from the waters of human history. It is called neo-paganism.

Neo-paganism is a belief in spirituality rather than religion and in technique rather than relationship. The neo-pagan isn't necessarily a dark demon worshipper and if he does offer ritual sacrifices in the accepted sense of the term it is more likely to be as a means of influencing energies rather than of pleasing the gods. Indeed, his spirituality has little to do with a transcendent God or gods. What he will acknowledge is that life is full of mystery and that the sum of all the life energies creates something greater than the whole. Thus he will reverence the earth and honour the connection between *material* and *Mater*, or Mother; he will treat nature as female and, in a non-personal sense, as God.

Our neo-pagan will embark on a journey to discover the spirituality within but how he does so will depend upon his temperament. He may perceive it as artistic sensibility, or ecological awareness, or the power of positive visualisation, or sexual vitality, or mystic union, or influence over others. Whatever the nature of the quest he will be eager to discover techniques to assist him in making it. These might range from pilgrimages to ancient sites of spirituality to creating a feng shui business environment. Amulets, meditation crystals, statuettes, sexual fetishes, essential oils – the whole array might be used to turn the cosmic force to his advantage. Such a person may advance with the help of a guru and may learn secret mantras, or spells. He will network with others of like mind and may go on to develop a cosmic or mystical connection that enables him to affect the psychological and physical condition of others. If he travels far enough he may aspire to become a materialist magician – in effect a secularised witch. C. S. Lewis anticipated this trend with remarkable insight when he wrote *The Screwtape Letters*: 'If once we can produce our perfect work – the Materialist Magician, the man, not using but veritably worshipping, what he vaguely calls "Forces" while denying the existence of "spirits" – then the end of the war will be in sight.'[7]

In this emerging worldview the concepts of right and wrong take on a different meaning to those of the past, for the scientist sees right and wrong in terms of the provability of a theory, the existentialist as the commitment or otherwise to a leap in the dark, and the Christian in terms of obedience or disobedience to the law of God. The scientist puts things right by revising his logic, the existentialist by taking courage, and the Christian by repentance and renewal. The neo-pagan is pragmatic. Did the technique work to further the cause of spiritual enlightenment? Did we network enough energy to produce good magic?

All this brings us to look at the worldview expressed in *Harry Potter*. To be fair to the author, this may or may not reflect her own view – these books are, after all, works of fiction – but they do reflect the trend in our post-Cold War, post-Christian, postmodern society. An important part of their appeal may lie in the measure to which they also reinforce the move towards neo-paganism. If so, we are dealing less with traditional witchcraft and more with spiritual secularism – though the latter will very likely cause us to regress to the former.

This is where comparisons with C. S. Lewis and J. R. R. Tolkien fail. Those authors wrote from a very different worldview. They also addressed a culture that still held to a Christian consensus and that accepted biblical moral and spiritual boundaries. The world today is much altered, as witness how Gandalf in *Lord of the Rings* could be hijacked by New Agers. The God of the Bible does not fit and cannot fit into the world of *Harry Potter*.

Typical of neo-paganism, Harry Potter makes his redemptive choices unaided by any higher Being. There is no inspiration from above, no Spirit of God at work. Indeed, his is a spiritless world, one that is coloured by the Western value of reason and technology, where manipulation can be taught like a school subject – a sort of secular shamanism where the moral choices have to do only with the end to which the shaman puts his power but not with the techniques themselves. This is spiritually dangerous since in attempting to manipulate what we think is no more than a force, we may fall foul of the purposes of both God and the devil.

In our humanistic arrogance we like to think we can control good and evil – a temptation as old as Eden – but in reality we can't. We need the help of God himself, and if we do not recognise that fact we may just find ourselves at the beck and call of the greatest power freak of all time. Let us make no mistake: however much we like to deny it, evil has an intelligent spirit behind it that we call Satan. That is why Jesus taught us to pray, 'Lead us not into temptation, but deliver us from the evil one.'

Here are some pertinent words for those who want to dabble in the realm of the spirits:

> There are two equal and opposite errors into which our race can fall about the devils. One is to disbelieve in their existence. The other is to believe, and to feel an excessive and unhealthy interest in them. They themselves are equally pleased with both errors and hail a materialist or a magician with the same delight.[8]

One of the unsavoury consequences of neo-paganism, with its emphasis on enlightenment and the mastery of spiritual techniques, is that it leads inevitably to elitism and class-ism.

Harry Potter is often excused because he is a special child, a protégé of the headmaster, Dumbledore. Only those portrayed as vindictive insist that he keeps the rules and takes his punishments. The 'enlightened' Dumbledore encourages by a secret alliance the bending of the rules. This elitism is only one aspect of the entire parallel culture, for Harry Potter's world consists of a secret society of arcane Gnostics with even their own school, bank and shops accessed by secret passwords and spells; a higher order of beings possessed of occult knowledge that grants them great advantages over lesser mortals. South African apartheid would have sat comfortably with such distinctions.

As a result, we are presented with some crude cultural stereotyping. Nowhere is this more apparent than in the portrayal of the revolting Dursley family. The Dursleys are selfish petty bourgeoisie, clueless irritants with 'a medieval attitude toward magic'. Yet, while their behaviour is inexcusable, their birth is not. Half of Britain is made up of ordinary middle-class people who through no fault of their own are holding down regular, if boring, jobs and living in ordinary suburban houses.

Maybe the Dursleys will come to recognise Harry Potter for who he is at the end and owe him some debt of gratitude, but outside of such compulsion to do so there can be no salvation for the Dursleys. They are Muggle born and bred and the rules of birth are everything.

What is true of the Dursleys is true of all Muggles. Unless you are one of the chosen there is no real life for you, just banal mediocrity. Since to be a witch is by birth, you cannot change and, if magic is a metaphor for spiritual values, there is no hope for you. You were born wrong. This select elect approach is the crassest form of elitism and mere mortals don't even get a look in. A Hindu caste system could not be more cruel. How different from Jesus who would be known as the Friend of Muggles, however much the elite Pharisees sneered at him!

A world based on such grim rules has no room for grace. It isn't then a very happy place. Although the children have fun, they appear not to have any inner joy. Harry

Potter's world is sour and sallow, oft-times bleak and brooding, hinting at evil and moral ambiguity. Anne McCain has likened it to the 'increasingly dark . . . tangled terrain and psychology of Batman movies'.[9] Elizabeth Mounce, addressing the South Carolina Board of Education says, 'The books have a serious tone of death, hate, lack of respect, and sheer evil.' Doomed by birth, we are at the mercy of a real and sinister evil, which all must fear.

It is noteworthy that the first *Harry Potter* book is written at the droll level of classic schoolboy humour that does much to debunk its seriousness. There is no real horror here, no build up of psychological tension to cause nightmares. It is Disney's *Sorcerer's Apprentice* stuff. But by the fourth volume all that has changed and the magic has become much more serious, with the promise of it becoming darker still in subsequent volumes. While we understand that the author intends her readers to grow along with Harry Potter as he progresses through school, does life have to become darker as we approach adulthood? Many of us find life improves considerably as we grow older. We should wonder at this pathological bleakness.

This was very much the world of old paganism in which the ancient Greco-Roman myths were framed, and in which redemption was hard to come by. Life was short-lived and fearful. Surrounded by nameless dreads, knowing not where they came from nor whence they would go, people turned to the occult adepts whose magic arts appeared to offer some solace against the vagaries of fate. It was small comfort.

However, deliverance was to come to the pagan world. One day an army of ordinary people, refusing to carry weapons yet capable of performing miracles, began to tell a new story wherever they travelled. It wasn't the tale of an awe-inducing wizard, nor of a misfit spear-wielding mercenary, nor of a super-zapping sky warrior, all of whom might be as terrifying as the enemies they had come to vanquish. Instead, it was the simple story of the day when God the Creator took the form of a baby, lived our life and died our death and, as sure as the turn of the season, rose again to give life to the world. It was the tale of innocent blood shed for the sins of the guilty, of the promise of life after death, of adoption into the love and grace of God. Such a message was already written in the natural order and hinted at in the myths of the past. It could transform the culture without abolishing it, so that the best would be purified and the worst removed. Needing no violence, it was embraced by Jews, Greeks, Romans, Persians and Celts alike because in the truest sense it was a better story.

6
A Better Story

Old world cultural Christianity may be finished in the West but the faith itself is as vibrant as ever. With roots older than time itself, it remains as fresh as an early summer's dawn and is on the brink of a significant resurgence. What a stark and cheerful contrast it makes to the bleak world of paganism where winter never quite ends and spring is for ever uncertain!

Rowling paints the pagan scene well. Christmas at Hogwarts celebrates light without the Light. It is a feast without the Guest, and gifts are given but the Gift is not received. Devoid of angels it is empty of praise, for no Saviour is born, no Baby fills the crib. We must live another year in the chill shadow of Voldemort.

Yet, in contrasting reality, 'to us a child is born, to us a son is given, and the government will be on his shoulders. And he will be called Wonderful Counsellor, Mighty God, Everlasting Father, Prince of Peace' (Isaiah 9:6).

Of all the great religious and secular systems in the world, only the Christian faith provides an adequate base for hope because only the Christian faith has a doctrine of grace and truth incarnated in Jesus of Nazareth, the Son of God. Only the Christian faith presents us with God revealing himself in terms that we can understand.

For Jesus isn't Superman or ET; he is our kind of man, feeling as we do, limited as we are, yet under the anointing of the Holy Spirit, demonstrating the reality of God's intervention in the pain and confusion of human experience. Who cannot wonder at the words and works of this man whose eyes could set your heart on fire, whose voice could still the storm and stir the soul, whose strong hands could heal the sick and raise the dead? Should we not follow the Good Shepherd who lays down his life for the sheep? For Jesus dies, the willing victim for others, tearing down the façade of religion, outfacing the satanic accuser with irrefutable righteousness, satisfying the most exacting demands for justice, and winning cynical hearts with the greatest demonstration of unconditional love ever shown.

Then God raises him from the dead. The Prince of Life arises victorious over the ultimate enemy to bring life and hope to all who believe and to break the shackles of deceitful night. Striding through the ranks of awed lesser powers he takes his place by right as Lord of all and receives the nations as his inheritance, whereupon, as Head of the church, he sends forth his Holy Spirit to announce through the lives, words and miracles of his people the forgiveness of sins, reconciliation with the Father, freedom from Satan's grip, and a life of endless transformation lived out in a community of grace.

True, this grace is often subverted by Christians them-selves into legalism and into licence, and truth is some-times reduced to opinion and ecclesiastical convenience, but these are errors. The truth that is Christ is incorruptible and all true seekers will find him.

This gospel comes with a universal appeal that excludes nobody from the offer of salvation. The voluntary humility of Jesus flies right in the face of proud human hierarchies. Jesus emptied himself of his rightful trinitarian equality with God to become like one of us – and lower – and that is why the gospel bars no one on the grounds of birth, gen-der, education or economic status. Witches and Muggles alike can be saved: 'You are all sons of God through faith in Christ Jesus, for all of you who were baptised into Christ have clothed yourselves with Christ. There is neither Jew nor Greek, slave nor free, male nor female, for you are all one in Christ Jesus' (Galatians 3:26–28). Sorry, you modern-day egalitarians, feminists and socialists. Jesus got there two thousand years before you and he did so without recourse to bitterness and violence, nor did he exchange one tyranny for another.

Not only does the gospel welcome everyone in on an equal footing, but it also gives everyone an equal access to the mystery of the faith: under the instruction of the Holy Spirit it is an open secret for all to explore. Spiritual growth is not a matter of mastering secret esoteric techniques but of developing a loving relationship with the Almighty: We 'grow in the grace and knowledge of our Lord and Saviour Jesus Christ' (2 Peter 3:18).

This means that true followers of Christ do not live by a set of carefully cultivated rules, complete with orders of merit, but by a living relationship with Jesus who truly 'fills full' the law of God. This relationship begins with an inner transformation so powerful that it can only be described as a spiritual rebirth, and it results in a life filled with the dynamic energy of the Holy Spirit and that progressively turns obedience to God's will into a living instinct of grace. Instead of treating the Sermon on the Mount as a new set of rules imposed from without, the believer discovers this law of love written on his heart so that it can be willingly lived out in love for God and love for our neighbours.

As such, the gospel message laid the foundations for true community and historically has provided the greatest incentive to enlightened civilisation, despite all the corruption and resistance of kings and politicians alike. It is to this gospel that we owe our democracies, our universal education, our health services and our social welfare institutions. This Christian God-spell, the truth Myth, by its own intrinsic power broke the cynicism and despair of the pagan world because it addressed the real needs of people with a real solution.

The trouble is, everyone wants what Christians have but without the message that makes it possible in the first place. The world is full of hypocrites! Political systems cannot produce what only grace has the power to do. At best they mimic it. Even less will neo-paganism succeed. That is why it is folly to suggest that because the *Harry Potter* myth has certain redeeming points and moral values it is somehow Christian. It just isn't. Modern paganism does, of course, recognise the reality of good and evil, but because it misunderstands the cause it cries out for no more than a hero. Heroism was considered by the pagan Greeks to be the greatest of virtues – something Jesus agreed with when he said that 'greater love has no-one than this, that he lay down his life for his friends' (John 15:13) – and Jesus himself is the greatest hero who ever lived. Yet we will have to go much further than *Harry Potter*. He may draw inspiration from his mother's love in his times of greatest need but he draws no inspiration from God. A mother's love to save her child is instinctive; by contrast, Jesus chose freely and with no other constraint than his love for sinners to lay down his life for us. That's real inspiration!

At the heart of the Christian gospel lies the death and resurrection of Christ. Jesus wasn't just a hero who beat up the devil or who inspired us to overcome the dark side of our psyches. He made atonement for us. This is the doctrine that modern-day pagans hate. To suggest that we need reconciliation by means of a blood sacrifice offends them because their world is one where everyone is good unless corrupted by others – a half-truth that adds up to a complete error! Like it or not, there is a fundamental and fatal ego bias in all of us that makes us want to be as gods without God. We have eaten from the wrong tree and it has poisoned us to death. That is why it took someone to die on a tree to bring us back to life.

As for you, you were dead in your transgressions and sins, in which you used to live when you followed the ways of this world and of the ruler of the kingdom of the air, the spirit who is now at work in those who are disobedient. All of us also lived among them at one time, gratifying the cravings of our sinful nature and following its desires and thoughts. Like the rest, we were by nature objects of wrath. But because of his great love for us, God, who is rich in mercy, made us alive with Christ even when we were dead in transgressions – it is by grace you have been saved. And God raised us up with Christ and seated us with him in the heavenly realms in Christ Jesus. (Ephesians 2:1–6)

This has to be the most positive psychology in the world, for it truly releases us from bondage to our past and it provides us with both the power and the presence of God to live for the future. Winter really does end and summertime begin.

The world of the Christian is one that brings to bear upon the sadnesses and corruptions of life the beautifying and energising grace of the Holy Spirit and the redemptive power of Christ. This is not a world of dark demons but a world of bright fellowship, of gifts granted freely and of grace generously bestowed. It engages us in a spiritual warfare but it does so with the help of a world of angels ministering on behalf of the elect. Sure there are demons and principalities and powers, and sometimes the battle is hard, but the victory is assured through the name of Jesus and the blood of Calvary.

To proclaim this message of grace is the mission calling and the task of the church. We are an apostolic community commissioned and empowered to announce the good news of Jesus Christ to every person on the planet without fear or favour. We have no need whatsoever to be ashamed of this message, for it carries God's power to transform lives and it does so today with ever-increasing effectiveness right across the globe.

The missionary church has met paganism many times in its history and has overcome it every time by refusing to use military power or deceit. Instead, we have told the simple story of Jesus, shown a defenceless love to all people, lived lives of joyful piety, and performed better miracles than the pagans. We have done all this out of profound gratitude to Jesus and with a persistent passion to see his gracious government established in the hearts and lives of men and women the world over. It is time to train a new generation for the unfinished task.

7
Train up a Child

Educating children in wisdom is a fundamental responsibility that we may not shirk. If we don't do it, someone else will attempt it, and unless we are very sure of their credentials and motives, we will be advised to take on the task ourselves.

Wisdom begins with protection. When my mother shielded my eyes from seeing the results of a horrific road accident at the age of four, she was quite right. That may sound like common sense, but it is amazing just how many parents allow their children to watch violent and sexually explicit content on the TV channels, and how many permit them unlimited access to the Internet, let alone caring not a bit about what they are reading. This is not only stupid it is downright irresponsible. As we pointed out earlier in this book, the images embedded in childhood do without doubt influence a child's later life. All parents, teachers and youth workers have a responsibility to exercise a degree of censorship over the material to which the children in their care are exposed, and that must include what goes on in the school classroom.

As cultural gatekeepers we must know when to exercise caution and when to impose an outright ban. Some material will never be appropriate because it is implicitly evil in intent and in content. Other material may depend upon the age and sensibility of the individual child. The fact that something is considered to be entertaining or 'everyone's reading it' is not in itself a sufficient justification for letting children participate.

That said, we should beware knee-jerk reactions. If we overreact for the wrong reasons, for example simply because of 'scare words' like 'witch' or 'ghost' in the title, our children are likely to consider us pathetic and out of touch. Once they lose respect for our judgement they will form their own, but without the experience of life that teaches us where the safe boundaries are. Or they may grow up paranoid, fearing to read or watch anything that doesn't have a cross or a holy pigeon on the cover in case they become contaminated. That may produce either reactionary bigots in adult life or those who kick over the traces once they discover the pleasure that has been denied them for so long.

Even if we do feel it right to ban certain materials from our children's cultural intake, let us make sure that they don't feel deprived or even punished. Provide something better instead. A good substitute is always better than a one-sided outright ban. A friend of ours, not approving of Pokémon for his eight-year-old son, asked him to dispose of the cards and explained why. After a few days of indecision, the boy did so. On the basis of the child's own choice, the father brought him a really decent football, much to the boy's delight.

Our task as Christians is to be proactive in the world. Instead of just reacting against everything we dislike, we are to propagate the better message of the gospel. Without shame, we should bring its values to bear on every aspect of our lives and the lives of our children. Censorship is not enough; we must teach our children to think and to discern the difference between good and evil, and to make good use of that acquired wisdom in furthering the faith within themselves and among their peers.

This is a learned process. The ability to discern between good and evil comes about by experience: 'Solid food is for the mature, who by constant use have trained themselves to distinguish good from evil' (Hebrews 5:14). We should not expect our children to become wise at one sitting! Nor does it come about by hard study – which may be a relief to some – but by the renewal of minds and bodies yielded to the Lord's service. If we are to train our children in wisdom, we must read and watch much of what they read and watch, and we must ensure that these matters are open season for discussion.

Harry Potter isn't the best starting point for younger children but with children of, say, eleven plus it does provide an opportunity to help them reflect morally and spiritually. Before that age there are many better stories that can provide good myth and adventure from a theistic and often Christian worldview. Not that we should be afraid to let our children read books written by non-Christians or books that do not have an explicit religious theme. Indeed, there is a good argument for keeping religious figures out of fairy tales so that there will be no doubt in children's minds that these are of a different order from salvation history. Father Christmas is fine as a fanciful story, but Father Christmas meets Jesus or the apostle Peter is confusing. Nor need God be mentioned explicitly; the worldview of the book may allow the character of God to shine through the players in the story.

Even pagan myths can reflect on reality. One of the reasons why the ancient Celts surrendered their beliefs in favour of Christianity was because they found that it provided the fulfilment of so much that their myths and traditions hoped for. Since we are considering a modern story written after the mythic pattern, even though we are far from Narnia, we can use *Harry Potter* as a means of helping our children gain discernment.

Harry Potter is set in a parallel world that interchanges and interacts with our own. This raises questions about the nature of reality. Is there an invisible world? Can we enter it? The film *The Matrix* portrays a parallel world in Platonist terms and it has got many students and adults thinking about an alternative to materialism. The Bible indicates at least three realms of reality: the visible world, the heavenly places, and the third heaven. We should encourage our children and teens to read the book of Revelation. They will not understand all the symbolism, but the book will open their eyes to a reality beyond the material and intellectual. This is the realm where Christ is seated in glory and where Christians, seated with him, share in his author-ity. It is also the amphitheatre where the spiritual war is fought. How much are your children aware of this as they study at school and college?

Conflict is a central theme in the *Harry Potter* tales, as it is also in the Bible. Yet whereas Harry Potter's world is dualistic – that is, good and evil are in equal contention – the Scriptures affirm that this world is ruled by a good Creator who himself is uncreated. God and the devil are not equal. Satan is but a creature; spiritual, but severely limited in his attributes. He cannot, like God, be every-where, know everything or do just anything. For this rea-son, children should not fear the devil. Instead, they should trust in the Lord and worship him for his goodness. You should take the opportunity to discuss good and evil with your children. It is a major concern. Rowling even introduces the death of a child into the fourth volume, pro-viding a chance to talk about that most taboo of subjects.

Harry Potter's world is full of taboos and rules. Such a place has little room for the relaxed open-heartedness of grace. Life clearly does have its dangers, but just how defensive should we be? Is there no place left for trust in this cynical world? Christians have always trusted that the Lord's angels will look after them. How relevant is this to your children in today's world?

It would be hard to avoid the connection between severe depression, mental breakdown and the Dementors as por-trayed by Joanne Rowling. Her coined term is not a long way removed from the word 'demented' – out of one's mind. Depression, suicide and breakdowns are tragically common among teenagers. Discuss with them why this is so and talk too about the reality of demons and angels. We have a better remedy than the Patronus proposed in the *Harry Potter* story. The comforts of Christ's victory, the help of the Holy Spirit, the Strengthener, and the vision of future glory are powerful weapons. Many of us, knowing the assault of evil, have found immense power in the name of Jesus. As for the illegal *cruciatus* curse in *Harry Potter*, what more powerful remedy exists than the deliverance wrought by the crucifixion of Christ?

The excellent virtue of love and loyalty among friends is prominent in *Harry Potter*, and it is tested and tried. Sometimes it is revealed to be false, and sometimes what appears to be false turns out to be remarkably true. Our children have to learn discernment when it comes to friendships. They must learn too the moral limits of loyalty. One of the follies of our modern media is to portray calf love as an infallible virtue, leading teenagers to rebel against all authority and good sense in its pursuit. Help your children to discern the difference between true love and immature obsession.

The love shown in *Harry Potter* is noble, but let's not make the silly mistake, as some churchmen have, of thereby describing this as Christian. Love between people is part of God's common grace in the world; we may not like it, but even Hitler loved his mistress, Eva Braun. Truly Christian love is of a different order. Jesus called us to love and to forgive even our enemies. To date, Harry Potter comes nowhere near such a grace. This raises very real issues for our children. What do you do about the school bully? How can you forgive those who maim innocent people?

Harry Potter is interested in the meaning of life and wants to explore his world. He is cautioned by his mentor, Dumbledore, that 'Curiosity is not a sin, but we should exercise caution with our curiosity'. What are the limits of curiosity? How far should we delve into the mysteries of science? Should we try taking drugs just to find out what it is like? This is an age that encourages experimentation, especially in the sexual realm, and it does so at an ever younger age. When are we ready for such experiences? The pressure upon many children is extreme and we must discuss with them where to set the limits.

There are many *Harry Potter* websites springing up. Most of these will be at the fun level but hyperlinks will point children to where they can learn 'real' magic. Web filters can be used to block explicit sex, violence and bad language, but not witchcraft. We need to caution our children about exploring these other sites.

Since these books are about witchcraft they raise the question: How shall we view witchcraft in today's world? We are told in *Harry Potter* that the school, Hogwarts, was built 'far from prying Muggle eyes, for it was an age when magic was feared by common people, and witches and wizards suffered much persecution'. The author is giving an opinion here that reflects on real history. It suggests that we should no longer fear witches and wizards since this is a more enlightened age. It's worth discussing why, and indeed to what extent, society persecuted witches in the past, and why people had such fears. While we would not wish to condone killing witches, is there still anything to fear? To what extent is it dangerous to engage in witchcraft? What are the possible consequences? Much of the *Harry Potter* witchcraft is far-fetched and quite humorous, but there is a definite serious side and the children at Hogwarts are being trained in its use. Moreover, some of those being trained are already known to be attracted to the Dark Side. What does that teach us about the dangers of dabbling in the occult?

It is too early to say whether Harry Potter will turn out to be a Messiah figure. He is more likely to become a shaman, a teenage pop hero with healing gifts. Whether he also dies and rises again, we will have to wait and see. In an age when children are taught that all religions are legitimate ways to God and that there is little difference between the holy man, the Dalai Lama, a shaman, a guru, Buddha, Mohammed and Jesus, we will want to stress the uniqueness of Jesus. He isn't simply the best player on the field; he is quite unique. Others might aspire to be called son of God by virtue of their spiritual achievements. Jesus was for ever the eternal Son of God who laid aside his glory and came for a while to live among us: 'Who, being in very nature God, did not consider equality with God something to be grasped, but made himself nothing, taking the very nature of a servant' (Philippians 2:6–7). The others try to climb up above the mass, whereas Jesus voluntarily came down to join us. The difference raises the question as to whether we save ourselves by our own works of self-improvements or whether we are saved by faith in Christ.

Jesus did his works by the power of the Holy Spirit, and

he calls each one of us to do the same. The shaman con-
nects with a spirit by means of channelling and often goes
into a trance in order to heal. The Christian seeks for the
anointing of the Holy Spirit to flow – a quite different
source! Our children can easily feel powerless in today's
world, yet they have power available to them in Christ.
The spiritual gifts of insight and healing are not just for
Christian meetings; they are for the real world of home,
school, college, workplace and sports club. We must
encourage and train our children in their use. The power
available to the Christian is released not through a desire
to control but through submission to the will of the Father.
So, Jesus did not come to please himself, but to do the will
of his Father who sent him.

Luke Skywalker in *Star Wars* abandons his trust in his
technical abilities and lets the Force take him over. Harry
Potter, in a similar manner, trusts his innate instincts rather
than the rules in times of crisis. This raises the question of
to what extent we should trust our innate feelings. Have
we relied too much on reason? What does it mean to let the
Holy Spirit work through us? Many Christians are afraid
of feelings and intuition because they have so little experience of the Holy Spirit in their lives. Instead, they live by
an unbiblical rationalist worldview that really cuts no ice
in a postmodern world. How much can we trust our
instincts and do they need tempering with reason? What is
the place of visions and symbols in the process of guid-
ance? How can our inexperienced youngsters get it right?

Harry Potter's instincts sometimes lead him to break the
school and moral rules. We may wish to discuss the place

of moral absolutes. What about telling white lies, for example, or stealing to help the poor? Is it justifiable to bomb innocent people because they are ruled by a dictator we don't like? When we use the same weapons as evil but for good purposes, as Harry Potter does, what does this tell us about means and ends? These are important questions.

Typical of a neo-pagan world there is a certain moral relativism in *Harry Potter*. Being cast as an alienated, autonomous figure, a misfit hero, Harry is sometimes foolish but never bad. His search, therefore, is not for moral and spiritual redemption but for wisdom. He will be saved by gnosis (special knowledge), not by washing. Any humility he shows will be only towards his gurus, as the chosen one has no need for repentance. This combination of his alienation and gifting makes him superior, especially over Muggles. Muggles don't even believe in magic (don't miss the word play 'Mugs all'). How does this make a Christian child feel in the playground when he is cast among the unbelievers by this arrogant elitism? Does this help him understand how other minorities feel? For at the heart of the Harry Potter stereotypes is the same mentality that produces the evils of racism, classism and sexism.

Since spell-casting plays such an important role in the *Harry Potter* books, we should encourage our children in the use of their own spiritual weapons. These are based upon the resounding defeat of Satan at Calvary where Jesus, 'having disarmed the powers and authorities . . . made a public spectacle of them, triumphing over them by the cross' (Colossians 2:15). This is the great spell that dispels all other spells! Thus, the warfare that we engage in is a mopping-up operation; the victory is already assured.

The Christian armour, as described in Ephesians 6:13–18, is all based upon this critical event. Regarding our two attacking weapons, the word of God and prayer, 'though we live in the world, we do not wage war as the world does. The weapons we fight with are not the weapons of the world. On the contrary, they have divine power to demolish strongholds. We demolish arguments and every pretension that sets itself up against the knowledge of God' (2 Corinthians 10:3–5). This being so, we must empower and equip our children in the spiritual use of these weapons.

Every Christian parent, youth worker and teacher needs to play their part in ensuring that the children in their charge are taught the Christian gospel and the worldview that flows from it. Our children should be trained to share the knowledge of the true and living God for themselves without any need to feel apologetic for their faith. They should be taught how to advise others to shun wrong behaviour and occult activity, without sounding holier-than-thou. We should help them discover their own spiritual gifts and how to use these for the blessing of others. Since Christian children and teenagers are often in a minority, we should encourage them to realise that 'the one who is in you is greater than the one who is in the world' (1 John 4:4). Teach them too the value of fellowship with other believers when they are in their secular environment.

In fighting this good fight of the faith, our children should be supplied with good scriptures and good prayers that address their common needs and that, under the anointing of the Holy Spirit, really do change the spiritual climate.

Conclusion

We set out to examine some of the most significant trends in our culture and the way they affect our children. In referring to the *Harry Potter* books we have tried to be even-handed and have left it to those with children to decide whether or not the books are suitable reading matter for their particular charges. This will not please everyone, but the alternative of a prescribed list of reading matter too easily absolves us from our responsibility to think for ourselves. Training up a child in the way he should go is not something we can pass on to others, least of all the secular media. It is our task and we must do it prayerfully and wisely.

Many forces, for good and ill, seek to bend and shape the minds of our children. Whether those minds finish up as beautiful living sculptures or as warped, distorted messes will depend very largely on the values that are embedded early on in their experience. The gospel of our Lord Jesus Christ and all works of art, science, literature and entertainment that encourage compassionate realism in our care for others, coupled with noble aspirations to be the people God intended us to be, can work together to produce a generation that is confident, robust, wise and merciful. May they be called the children of the resurgence and may they change the world.

Notes

1. Karen Jo Gounaud, 'Should Harry Potter go to public school?', *Family Friendly Libraries*, October 1999.
2. Lindy Beam, 'Plugged in – What shall we do with Harry?', *Focus on the Family*, July 2000.
3. *USA Weekend*, 12–14 November 1999.
4. John Houghton, *The Oswain Tales* (Kingsway Publications, 2001).
5. Aldous Huxley, *The Doors of Perception* (Flamingo, 1994).
6. John Andrew Murray, *Teachers in Focus*.
7. C. S. Lewis, *The Screwtape Letters* (Fount, 1998).
8. *Ibid*.
9. Anne McCain, *World on the Web*, 30 October 1999.

Appendix

The *Harry Potter* series to date

Harry Potter and the Philosopher's Stone
Harry Potter and the Chamber of Secrets
Harry Potter and the Prisoner of Azkaban
Harry Potter and the Goblet of Fire

Some *Harry Potter* names and places

Dementors	– state torturers
Diagon Alley	– the witches' street in London
Dobby	– a liberated house elf
Dumbledore	– the headmaster
Dursleys	– Harry's Muggle guardians
Fudge	– Ministry of Magic official
Ginny	– Ron's younger sister
Gringotts	– the Goblin bank

Hagrid	– a soppy giant
Harry Potter	– the hero
Hermione Granger	– a swot
Hogsmeade	– the local witches' village
Hogwarts	– the school of wizardry
Malfoy	– school sneak
McGonagall	– head of Gryffindor House
Mudbloods	– wizards with one Muggle parent
Muggles	– non-wizards
Quidditch	– an aerial sport
Ron Weasley	– Harry's pal
Sirius	– Harry's godfather
Snape	– head of Slytherin House
Voldemort	– the dark lord

Buying and Selling the Souls of Our Children

A Closer Look at Pokémon

by John Paul Jackson

Can you feel God's heart breaking?

Children of destiny are being enticed and lured by the spirit of the age. Some have drifted unknowingly into the realm of darkness. Will our sons and daughters accomplish their God-given mandate for this hour? Or will they become a lost generation? Someone must rise up and sound the alarm.

'I highly recommend this book.' – Wesley Campbell

'Read! Be warned! Be equipped.' – Lou Engle

'A warning that we all need to hear.' – Jack Taylor

JOHN PAUL JACKSON is founder of Streams Ministries International. He travels extensively around the world teaching on the art of hearing God, dreams, visions and the supernatural.

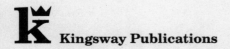

Kingsway Publications

A Closer Look at Science Fiction

by Anthony Thacker

Is the truth really out there?

Science fiction is one of the foremost ways in which our culture tries to explore creative possibilities and grapple with the big issues of life:

- Why do we exist?

- How do we handle our increasing power over the mechanics of life?

- What if we're not alone in the universe?

- Where does evil come from?

Anthony Thacker looks at the popular face of science fiction, and addresses the key *spiritual* and *moral* themes raised, especially by some of TV's most popular series.

K Kingsway Publications